THE FIGHT AGAINST
WAR AND
TERRORISM

By Jilly Hunt

ADLINES BEYOND THE HEADLINES BEYOND THE HEAD

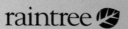

raintree

a Capstone company — publishers for children

Raintree is an imprint of Capstone Global Library Limited, a company incorporated in England and Wales having its registered office at 7 Pilgrim Street, London, EC4V 6LB – Registered company number: 6695582

www.raintreepublishers.co.uk
myorders@raintreepublishers.co.uk

Edited by Adrian Vigliano
Designed by Philippa Jenkins
Original illustrations © Capstone Global Library Limited 2017
Illustrated by Oxford Designers and Illustrators
Picture research by Morgan Walters
Production by Tori Abraham
Originated by Capstone Global Library Ltd
Printed and bound in China

ISBN 978 1 4747 4919 0
21 20 19 18 17
10 9 8 7 6 5 4 3 2 1

British Library Cataloguing in Publication Data
A full catalogue record for this book is available from the British Library.

Acknowledgements
We would like to thank the following for permission to reproduce photographs: Alamy: Euan Cherry, 39, Martyn Evans, 32, PA Images, 38, Stocktrek Images, Inc, 25; Capstone Press: Philippa Jenkins, map 1, 14, ipad 11, 12, 15, 18, 25, 26, 27, 33, 34, 37, 43; Getty Images: BERTRAND GUAY, (eiffel tower) Cover, Keystone-France, 36, MARWAN IBRAHIM, 31, MOHAMMED SAWAF, 23, Per-Anders Pettersson, 37, Peter Macdiarmid, 28, Sergei Savostyanov, 33; iStockphoto: danhowl, 26, Fbhenrg, 43; Newscom: akg-images, 9, ALI HAIDER/EPA, 22, ANJA NIEDRINGHAUS/EPA, 15, Davis/TNS, 30, Jerry_Lampen/epa, 21, JON SANTA CRUZ/KRT, 6, Kyodo, 20, Pacific Press/Sipa USA, 35, Pictures From History, 13, 17, Underwood Archives/UIG Universal Images Group, 16, yslb pak Xinhua News Agency, 29; Shutterstock: Asisyaj, 11, BravoKiloVideo, 27, Cako, design element, chairoij, 41, Dmytro Surkov, 42, Everett Historical, 4, 8, 10, 12, 34, Hang Dinh, 7, Lucky Team Studio, 40, Rommel Canlas, 1, Tooykrub, 19, Travel Stock, 24, ZoranOrcik, (buildings) Cover

We would like to thank Michael Doidge, Military Historian, for his invaluable help in the preparation of this book.

Every effort has been made to contact copyright holders of material reproduced in this book. Any omissions will be rectified in subsequent printings if notice is given to the publisher.

CONTENTS

Some words are shown in bold, **like this**. You can find out what they mean by looking in the glossary.

Chapter 1

WHAT'S BEYOND THE HEADLINES ABOUT WAR AND TERRORISM?

"CONCERN FOR CIVILIANS IN LATEST CIVIL WAR"

"HUNDREDS KILLED IN TERROR ATTACK"

"WAR DECLARED"

We've all seen headlines like this about war and terrorism. But how much do we really know about these issues?

War comes in different forms. War is armed and violent conflict among groups with opposing ideas. It can be local, such as between different tribal groups. It can also be an international fight between two or more nations of the world. Civil war is when different groups within the same country fight each other. Just as violence happens in war, terrorists also often use violence, but terrorists use it in a planned away against ordinary people. Terrorists try to frighten and control people through violence.

After World War II, people celebrated, hoping that there would never be another conflict like it.

The reasons for war

The reasons behind wars are often complicated and can date back to disagreements held centuries ago. Reasons for war include differences in political or religious beliefs. Sometimes the reason for war might be a disagreement over territory, with countries fighting about who owns an area of land.

Civil war happens when a group disagrees with the current political situation or the ruling party. Sometimes, it might be difficult to tell the difference between civil war and terrorism. In March 2011, protesters challenged Syrian President Bashar al-Assad. They were unhappy about the way his government was ruling the country. The government used violence to try to stop the protestors — an act of state terrorism. The situation in Syria got much worse and turned into a very complicated civil war.

Other countries that disagreed with each other seemed to be using Syria's war as their own battleground. They did this by providing support to the Syrian government or the rebels.

Key dates of significant wars in the 20th and 21st Centuries

1914–1918	World War I
1919–1921	Irish War of Independence
1922–1923	Irish Civil War
1936–1939	Spanish Civil War
1939–1945	World War II
1950–1953	Korean War
1954–1975	Vietnam War
1968–1998	The Troubles in Ireland
1982	Falklands War
1990–1991	Gulf War
1992–1995	Bosnian War
1998–1999	Kosovo War
2001–2014	War in Afghanistan
2003–2011	Iraq War and Insurgency
2011–present	Syrian Civil War

GOOD NEWS

Swedish historian Johan Norberg has some good news about war. He says the "risk of being caught up in a war, subjected to a dictatorship, or of dying in a natural disaster is smaller than it ever was".

The causes of terrorism

As with war, the reasons for terrorism also vary. Terrorist acts usually have a few things in common. They are often premeditated (planned) and occur without warning. Terrorist acts usually happen in public spaces and are intended to cause harm and spread fear.

The terrorist bombing of a commuter train in Madrid in 2004 killed 191 people.

Terrorists usually see themselves as different to those they are fighting. Some terrorist groups start because their members want to form a state. Many terrorists desire a state built on their own religious beliefs or **ideology**. For example, groups such as al-Qaida and ISIL have stated their desire to form Islamic states according to their beliefs. Others such as ETA (the Basque Fatherland and Liberty) in Spain and LTTE (the Liberation Tigers of Tamil Eelam) in Sri Lanka want their regions to become independent states.

Other groups are founded on hate and terrorize certain groups of people because of their race or religion. For example, neo-Nazi groups think white people are superior and should have more rights than other races and religions. They also believe in discriminating against different races and religion.

When a person agrees with a terrorist group but takes action without direction from that group, they are called a "lone wolf". Lone-wolf attacks represented 70 per cent of the deaths caused by terror attacks in the West between 2006 and 2015.

DID YOU KNOW?

Most terrorist acts happen in one of five countries: Iraq, Nigeria, Afghanistan, Pakistan and Syria.

Two brothers acting on their own were responsible for the bombings at the 2013 Boston Marathon which killed 3 people and injured 264 others. This photo shows a memorial for the victims. ▼

Chapter 2

WHAT'S BEYOND THE HEADLINES ABOUT WORLD WARS?

World War I

There have been many wars throughout the history of humanity. But **World War I (WWI)** (1914–1918) changed the way future wars were fought.

World War I involved many countries. On one side were the Central Powers, made up of Germany, Austria-Hungary, Turkey and Bulgaria. On the other were the Allies — France, Belgium, Luxembourg, the United Kingdom, Russia, Italy, Japan, Romania, Portugal, Greece and the US.

German soldiers on duty in a ▲ trench during World War I.

Technology in war

In the west of Europe, WWI was mainly fought in the **trenches**. Huge numbers of soldiers and weapons meant that trench warfare happened on a larger scale than ever before. However, both sides found that they weren't making much progress with trench warfare. Because of this, they tried to win by having the best technology. For example, each side tried to develop the best machine guns. Then in response to better machine guns on both sides, they tried to develop better armoured vehicles.

Taking to the air

Armies took to the air to try to learn more about the enemy. A new type of photographic film and wireless communication aided the crews. Both sides began developing more sophisticated aircraft. Bombs were dropped over cities such as London and Paris as WWI saw the start of "total war". This is the idea that all of a nation's resources, such as its factories, farms and its **civilians**, are open to attack.

WWI came to an end in 1918 as the Central Powers finally agreed a truce with the Allies.

GOOD NEWS

In 1920, the League of Nations was formed in an attempt to keep world peace. The League didn't prevent the events of **World War II (WWII) (1939–1945)** happening. But it did help countries to stabilize their finances and brought relief to the victims of war.

World War II

There were attempts to keep peace around the world after WWI. But within 20 years of WWI's end, a second world war had begun in Europe. By its end in 1945, WWII involved nearly every part of the world. On one side were the Axis powers, which included Germany, Italy and Japan. On the other were the Allies, which included France, Britain, the US and the **Soviet Union**.

▲ Hitler committed suicide on 30 April 1945 to avoid being captured by the Soviets.

A brief summary

World War II was triggered by Germany's invasion of Poland on 1 September 1939. Adolf Hitler, Germany's leader, had already taken over Austria and areas of Czechoslovakia. He wanted to make Germany (and himself) powerful by controlling more territory. As Hitler gained more powers, he made himself a **dictator** and used violence to suppress any opposition. He had a secret police force called the Gestapo that spread fear amongst the people in Germany's territories.

Inciting hatred

Hitler hated the mix of cultures that he experienced while growing up in Austria. Once he had power, he encouraged racial hatred, especially against Jews. He also encouraged hatred against Roma, Slavic peoples, homosexuals and disabled people. This hatred led to the killing of millions of people, an event known as the Holocaust. We now call an attempt to destroy a national or **ethnic** group "genocide" but the term didn't exist before 1944.

DID YOU KNOW?

The word *genocide* is formed from the Greek word *geno* meaning "race" and the Latin word *cide* meaning "killing". It was first used to describe the Nazis' attempts to destroy the Jewish race.

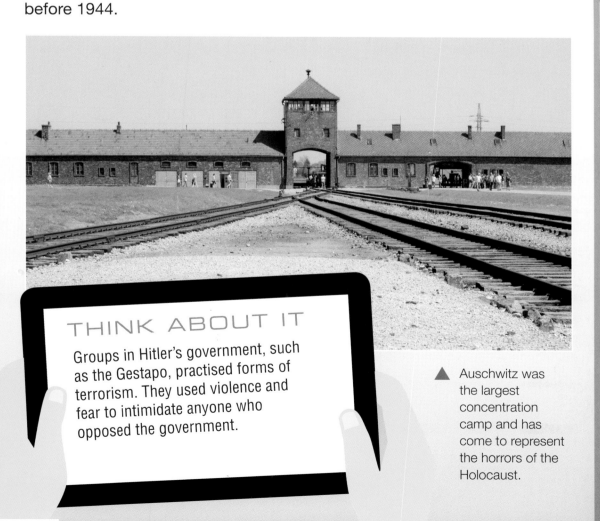

THINK ABOUT IT

Groups in Hitler's government, such as the Gestapo, practised forms of terrorism. They used violence and fear to intimidate anyone who opposed the government.

▲ Auschwitz was the largest concentration camp and has come to represent the horrors of the Holocaust.

The atomic bomb

Two Jewish scientists who fled to Britain helped to bring an end to WWII. Otto Frisch and Rudolph Peierls joined other scientists in the US-led Manhattan Project. Project scientists realized it might be possible to create an **atomic bomb**. This bomb would have an explosion equivalent to "several thousands tons of dynamite".They thought it was possible to make this powerful bomb small enough to fit in a plane. Manhattan Project scientists succeeded in developing the first **nuclear weapons**.

THINK ABOUT IT

The use of these two atomic bombs has remained controversial. Some argue that their use saved many lives by ending WWII. Others argue that it was wrong to use these bombs despite knowing that huge numbers of civilians would be killed.

The devastation caused by the atomic bomb affected huge numbers of civilians, including children. Those near the centre of the blast died immediately. Those further away suffered burns and illnesses caused by exposure to radiation.

A turning point for the world

On 6 August 1945, a US plane, *Enola Gay*, dropped an atomic bomb on Hiroshima, Japan. Hiroshima was a major centre for military equipment and weapons. The explosion had devastating and long-lasting effects. The bomb destroyed about 60 per cent of the city. However, Japan did not surrender. The US dropped a second, larger atomic bomb on Nagasaki, Japan, on 9 August 1945. The Japanese emperor asked for peace the next day. Soon after, Japan unconditionally surrendered.

Lessons learned

The dramatic images and tragic tales from survivors serve as a reminder of the destruction possible with atomic power. Experts predict that if a nuclear weapon were to be used again, millions of people would be killed or injured. The world's climate would likely be affected, leading to possible famines. World economies could also be affected, making it impossible for governments to provide aid. The world's nations need to continue to work together to prevent future use of nuclear weapons.

NATO

Following WWII, a division grew between the former Allies. The British Prime Minister, Sir Winston Churchill, described this situation in Europe. He said that "an iron curtain had descended". This meant that the west of Europe had been divided from the east by an imaginary barrier. The east became known as the Eastern or Soviet bloc. It included the Soviet Union, Poland, Romania, Bulgaria, Czechoslovakia and East Germany.

NATO member countries from 1949

1949
Belgium
Canada
Denmark
France
Iceland
Italy
Luxembourg
Netherlands
Norway
Portugal
United Kingdom
United States

1952
Greece
Turkey

1955
Federal Republic
of Germany

1999
Czech Republic
Hungary
Poland

2004
Bulgaria
Estonia
Latvia
Lithuania
Romania
Slovakia
Slovenia

2009
Albania
Croatia

The Soviet bloc governments were **Communist**. Communist governments held different political beliefs from those held by governments in the **democratic** west. Western leaders were worried that Communism would spread throughout the world. They also worried about the military power that the Soviet Union was building up. In 1949, the US, Canada and 10 European countries formed an alliance called the North Atlantic Treaty Organization (NATO). The NATO countries agreed that they were stronger together. They agreed that "an armed attack against one or more of them . . . shall be considered an attack against them all."

The collapse of the Soviet Union

With the collapse of the Soviet Union in 1991, NATO's role changed. It continues to provide defence against security threats. It also has a police-like role, attempting to prevent ethnic wars and terrorism and maintain peace. NATO also works alongside the **United Nations (UN)** in a peacekeeping role, managing matters such as refugee crises.

DID YOU KNOW?

After the 9/11 terrorist attacks on the US in 2001, NATO members agreed to fight terrorism together.

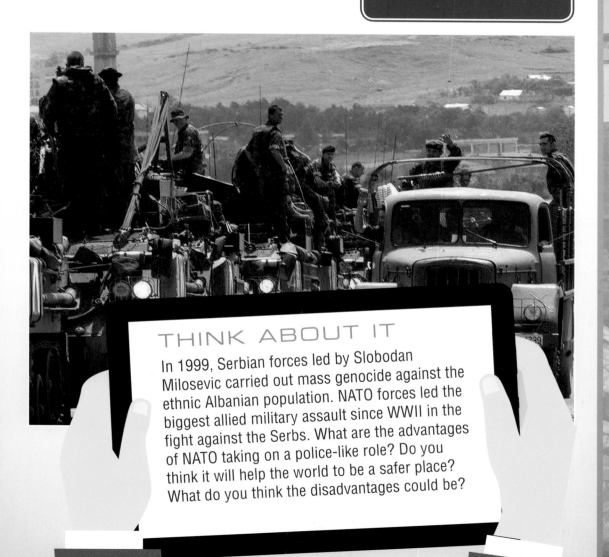

THINK ABOUT IT

In 1999, Serbian forces led by Slobodan Milosevic carried out mass genocide against the ethnic Albanian population. NATO forces led the biggest allied military assault since WWII in the fight against the Serbs. What are the advantages of NATO taking on a police-like role? Do you think it will help the world to be a safer place? What do you think the disadvantages could be?

Cold War

The Cold War is the name given to the post-WWII rivalry between the US and the Soviet Union. These superpowers fought together to defeat Germany during WWII. But after the war they were wary of each other and their alliance quickly collapsed.

The leaders of the United Kingdom, US and Soviet Union met as allies during WWII.

Stalemate

The relationship between these two countries was difficult. Each side seemed to be playing a strategic game and trying to outmanoeuvre the other. The two countries competed to build the strongest collection of nuclear weapons. The threat of a nuclear attack hung over each side should they make the wrong move. Neither side really wanted to use their nuclear weapons. Instead of fighting each other directly, they supported opposing sides in other countries' civil wars. The Korean War (1950–1953) and the Vietnam War (1955–1975) are both examples of this.

The closest the superpowers came to fighting each other was during the Cuban Missile Crisis in 1962. In order to defend Cuba, the Soviet Union installed nuclear missiles there. Because Cuba is so close to the US, the Soviet missiles presented a new Cold War threat. If launched, these missiles could reach the eastern coast of the US within minutes. Several tense days followed. Finally, Soviet premier Nikita Khrushchev agreed to remove the missiles. In return, the US promised to never invade Cuba.

In the Vietnam War, communist North Vietnam ▲ fought against the government of Southern Vietnam. Communist countries such as the People's Republic of China and the Soviet Union supported North Vietnam. Anti-communist countries, such as the United States, supported Southern Vietnam.

Chapter 3

WHAT'S BEYOND THE HEADLINES ABOUT PEACEKEEPING?

The United Nations

One of the positives that followed WWII was a new desire for world peace. Huge numbers of people were affected by both world wars. The League of Nations had failed to keep world peace. Countries around the world were keen to find an alternative.

On 24 October 1945, 50 countries formed the United Nations (UN). There are now 193 member states. The UN works to:

- maintain international peace and security
- promote sustainable development
- protect human rights
- uphold international law
- deliver humanitarian aid.

The UN has rules about the way nations are expected to act. For example, it says that any international disputes should be settled peacefully. It also says that nations should not use force or the threat of force against other nations.

GOOD NEWS

The UN's efforts at peacekeeping have helped reduce the number of people dying in conflicts since 1945.

On 1 January 2017, Antonio Guterres became the UN's Secretary-General, taking over from Ban Ki-moon. Guterres said that he believes:

"the international community's first priority is to be able to end [the conflict in Syria]" and *"to try to address all the other conflicts that are interlinked"*.

UN successes

It is generally thought that the world is a safer place because of the international co-operation that the UN encourages. The UN have worked to eliminate old mine fields, and to clear out munitions from past wars. They have worked toward the elimination of nuclear weapons, and in banning the testing of nuclear weapons. It is quite remarkable that countries have willingly given up their nuclear weapons. Yet that is what South Africa did after **Apartheid**, and Kazakhstan did after the collapse of the Soviet Union. There are also UN agreements in place for nuclear-weapon-free zones. Countries keep details of their defences top secret, but some agree to let the UN inspect their nuclear weapons.

The sculpture outside the UN headquarters in New York is called "Non Violence". ▼

Peacekeeping role played by the UN

The best way to keep the peace is to prevent conflicts from actually happening. The UN plays an important part in trying to prevent international arguments from progressing too far. It does this by acting as a neutral party to help nations resolve their differences.

DID YOU KNOW?

The UN currently has 16 peacekeeping operations underway in countries such as Syria, Haiti, Darfur, Liberia, Kosovo and Lebanon.

These Japanese soldiers are serving as UN Peacekeepers in South Sudan in 2016. ▼

DID YOU KNOW?

The UN has not always been successful with its peacekeeping missions. For example, corruption within the UN led to the massacre of 8,000 Bosnian Muslims in a UN "safe zone" in Srebrenica in 1995.

The UN also plays an important part in building peace once a conflict is over. An area is less likely to return to conflict if peace brings local people a better quality of life. So the UN works to promote sustainable development. This means working to provide for a community's well-being. Sustainable development can create new job opportunities, improved health care, and an environment that is protected.

Supporting refugees

Helping refugees and migrants remains one of the greatest challenges facing the world today. Refugees and migrants make dangerous journeys away from their homes to try to find safety. The UN works to ensure better treatment for these people and to provide aid for them.

Prosecuting war crimes

Part of keeping the peace is bringing justice to leaders who have committed crimes against their people. The UN operates an international court where leaders who have committed crimes are tried. A number of high-profile modern leaders have been put on trial. One example is former Serbian President Slobodan Milosevic. He was accused of war crimes, crimes against humanity and genocide. Milosevic died in prison before his trial could be completed.

Former Serbian leader Slobodan ▲ Milosevic, on trial at the UN's international court in 2001.

21

The UN's role in Iraq

In 2003, the UN agreed to support the government and people of Iraq. Iraq needed to rebuild following the overthrow of its leader, Saddam Hussein. The country needed help to set up a legal system, a system of voting and in encouraging human rights.

▲ Iraqis celebrate the fall of Saddam Hussein by beating a statue of him with their shoes.

A challenging role

The peacekeeping role that the UN undertakes is a challenging one. The UN is only as strong as the nations who contribute to those efforts. UN peacekeeping forces are made up of troops from many countries. They are not structured or equipped to deal with fighting. Their priority is to try to maintain peace. The UN role in Iraq was especially challenging. A US-led **coalition** had succeeded in removing Iraq's dictator, Hussein. But Hussein's overthrow left an opportunity for extremist groups such as al-Qaida and ISIL to seize power. Further battles in 2004 were fierce and fuelled by scandals of prisoner abuse by US soldiers at Abu Ghraib prison. Control of Iraq was handed over to a temporary Iraqi government in June 2004. But troops remained to try to keep the country secure. Peace seemed unlikely as terrorist groups used bombs and explosives against security forces and civilians.

The UN is working with 180 humanitarian partners to deliver the large amount of aid needed in Iraq.

The UN sees the humanitarian crisis in Iraq as one of the largest and most complex in the world. It says that 10 million people need aid and that this number may continue to rise.

DID YOU KNOW?

UN peacekeeping forces wear bright blue hats so that they can be clearly distinguished from other military. The UN pays £800 ($1,000) per soldier per month.

GOOD NEWS

Despite the dangers, the UN and its partners provide more than two million Iraqis with aid every month.

Chapter 4

WHAT'S BEYOND THE HEADLINES ABOUT INTERNATIONAL TERRORISM?

Trends in terrorism are changing, so the fight against terrorists must adapt too. In the past, most terrorist attacks were "home-grown" and happened in the terrorists' own country. In 2015, over 90 per cent of all the deaths from terrorism were in countries that were already in conflict. But terrorist activity, especially that of Islamic extremist groups, has become more international. Attacks have happened in many countries, including France, Spain, the UK and the US. Every nation needs to protect itself. This can make nations think only about their own safety and make international co-operation harder.

DID YOU KNOW?

Unless you live in a country in conflict, the chance of being involved in a terrorist incident is relatively low. It has been compared by some as roughly equivalent to the chance of drowning in your own bath.

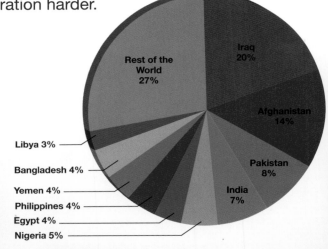

Iraq 20%

Rest of the World 27%

Afghanistan 14%

Libya 3%

Bangladesh 4%

Pakistan 8%

Yemen 4%

India 7%

Philippines 4%

Egypt 4%

Nigeria 5%

▲ This chart shows where terror attacks happened, by percentage, around the world in 2015.

◄ The Taliban introduced strict laws that reduced the freedom of women.

Deadliest groups

At the moment, four terrorist groups are considered the most deadly, based on the numbers they've killed. These are ISIL, Boko Haram, the Taliban and al-Qaida. All four are considered Islamic extremist groups. This means members of these groups consider themselves to be Muslims. Unlike the majority of Muslims, they think it is acceptable to use violence to achieve their aims.

Islamic extremists believe that western society and **globalism** are immoral and godless. They believe that anyone who doesn't think the way they do needs to either convert or be killed. They want to create Islamic states (or caliphates) where people would live by strict religious laws.

The terrain in Afghanistan ▲ challenged troops.

THINK ABOUT IT

Research has shown that terrorist activity is more likely to happen in countries where certain factors exist. Some of these factors include high youth unemployment, high levels of crime and access to weapons, and distrust in voting systems. If young people feel that they haven't got much future, they may want to revolt to try to change things. What do you think?

Why did 9/11 happen?

On 11 September 2001, four linked terror attacks organized by al-Qaida took place in the US. Two hijacked planes were deliberately crashed into the Twin Towers of the World Trade Center in New York. A third plane crashed into the Pentagon, the headquarters of the US Department of Defense. A fourth hijacked plane is thought to have been heading for the White House but crashed near Pittsburgh.

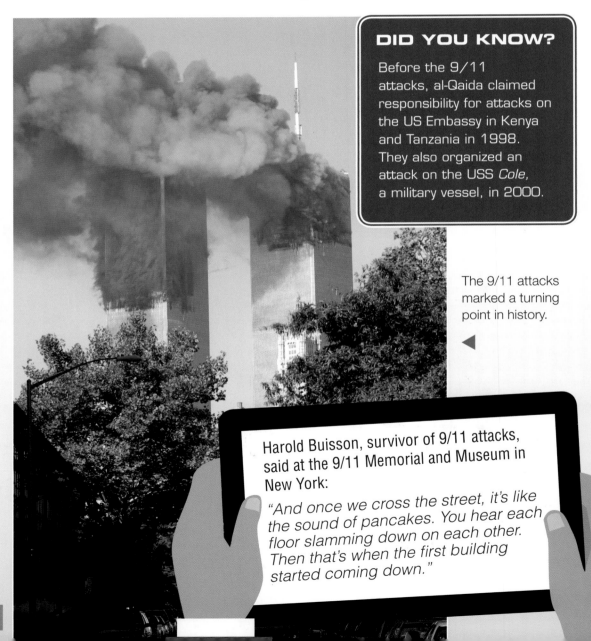

DID YOU KNOW?

Before the 9/11 attacks, al-Qaida claimed responsibility for attacks on the US Embassy in Kenya and Tanzania in 1998. They also organized an attack on the USS *Cole*, a military vessel, in 2000.

The 9/11 attacks marked a turning point in history.

◄

Harold Buisson, survivor of 9/11 attacks, said at the 9/11 Memorial and Museum in New York:

"And once we cross the street, it's like the sound of pancakes. You hear each floor slamming down on each other. Then that's when the first building started coming down."

Spreading fear

Al-Qaida's choice of targets was symbolic. To them, the World Trade Center represented globalization, freedom, decadence and corruption. The World Trade Center was also a source of economic power. Al-Qaida viewed these things as immoral. They knew they didn't have the resources to defeat the US military but they could still cause fear by attacking the Pentagon. By targeting the White House, they were aiming at the US government. Al-Qaida wanted to weaken the US and force the US government to reduce its involvement in the Middle East.

Many people had never heard of al-Qaida before the horrific 9/11 attacks. But the group was formed in 1988 by Osama bin Laden and Abdullah Azzam during the Soviet war in Afghanistan. Their aim was to overthrow governments in the Middle East and create a strict religious society. Initially, the groups focused on attacks closer to home but over time they changed their strategy to target the "far enemy" of the United States.

In the spot where the Twin Towers once stood is now a memorial to all the people who lost their lives in this tragic event.

US President George W. Bush, 2001:

"Any nation that continues to harbor or support terrorism will be regarded by the United States as a hostile regime."

The hunt for Osama bin Laden

Al-Qaida was based in Afghanistan, which was controlled by the Taliban in 2001. The US believed that the Taliban supported al-Qaida. They demanded that the Taliban hand over al-Qaida members and close their training camps. The Taliban refused, which led to the US forming a coalition to fight terrorism in countries around the world.

The 2005 terror ▲ attacks on London were a powerful reminder as to just how important it was to capture bin Laden.

THINK ABOUT IT

On 7 July 2005, al-Qaida launched another attack on the far enemy. Suicide bombers triggered three devices on the London Underground and one on a London bus. It was the worst terrorist attack on British soil. The explosions killed 52 people and injured hundreds of others.

Osama bin Laden became the world's most sought-after terrorist, although he managed to avoid capture for 10 years. The problem was that no one really knew where to start looking for him. Initially, the US-led coalition focused their military efforts on defeating the Taliban with two months of bombing. Then, special forces soldiers and **CIA** operatives started to track down bin Laden. They located him in a cave and bunker system that was made during the war against the Soviets in Afghanistan. But this was his territory and he knew where to hide. With the US getting closer, bin Laden and his fighters fled into Pakistan and some into Iran. In Pakistan, bin Laden was protected by local tribal groups.

Caught at last

Al-Qaida members knew it was risky to use technology to communicate. So they used couriers to deliver hand-written notes. Eventually, the CIA tracked down a key al-Qaida courier and his brother. They were surprised to find a compound much larger than the surrounding buildings. They knew someone important must live there. The CIA learned the brothers were living there with a family that fit the description of the bin Ladens. Osama bin Laden was killed by US Navy Seals on 29 April 2011.

DID YOU KNOW?

Khalid Sheikh Mohammed is frequently described as the "mastermind" of the 9/11 attacks. He has confessed to playing a part in 30 terrorist plots and was captured in Pakistan in 2003.

People gather outside the compound where bin Laden had hidden for years. ▶

The rise of ISIL

The Islamic extremist group, ISIL, is based in Syria and Iraq. ISIL has connections with other terrorist groups, notably the Nigerian-based Boko Haram. ISIL is also known by other names, such as Islamic State, ISIS, or Daesh. ISIL has a strong military presence and controls areas of Iraq and Syria. It has organized or encouraged terrorist attacks in the US, France, Belgium, Australia, Bangladesh and Indonesia. In 2016, the UN described the setbacks ISIL has experienced due to military efforts by international troops. However, it warns that ISIL are trying to expand, especially into South-East Asia, Yemen and Somalia. It states that countries in this region have introduced counter-terrorism strategies that are continually updated.

GOOD NEWS

In November 2016, an ISIL plot to attack targets in Paris was foiled. Five suspects appeared before an anti-terrorist judge.

- ■ ISIL controlled
- ■ Under attack by ISIL
- ▨ No opposition to ISIL

Mosul

Iraqi Kurdistan

Syria

Beirut

SYRIA

Damascus

LEBANON

Fallujah

Baghdad

DETAIL AREA

IRAN

EGYPT   SAUDI ARABIA

IRAQ

ISIL wants to create a large Islamic state where strict religious laws would be enforced.

GOOD NEWS

Six hundred women who escaped ISIL slavery are taking part in military training. They hope to use their knowledge of ISIL terrorist bases to protect people and to free remaining slaves.

People have described living under ISIL as like "living in a giant prison". ▼

Women under ISIL

Muslim women in ISIL-controlled areas live with very strict restrictions. They are not allowed to leave the house without a male guardian. They are forced to wear clothes that completely cover their bodies, including face veils that are double-layered. Women and their guardians are beaten and punished if they do not follow these rules. Women who aren't Muslims and who are captured by ISIL are treated as slaves.

The use of technology in terrorism

Technology plays a key part in terrorism and **counterterrorism**. Terrorists now include cyber terrorism as one of their weapons. This is when a terrorist aims to destroy a target's electronic system to stop them functioning properly. Governments around the world are investing a lot of money to make their systems more secure against cyber terrorism. Terrorists use techniques that make it harder for authorities to track them and remove their websites.

ISIL are known for their use of the internet and social media. They use these tools to recruit followers, post propaganda, raise funds and buy weapons. Experts estimate that since 2011, more than 40,000 people have come from over 120 different countries to fight with ISIL in Syria and Iraq.

▲ ISIL fighters are often well educated and many have strong technology skills.

The use of drones by militaries and governments has caused controversy.

◀

Use of technology to fight terrorists

The global coalition fighting terrorist groups is using the latest technology to monitor the groups and gain information. Surveillance aircraft or drones help them to see what is happening on the ground. This information can be quickly passed to troops on the ground to take action. Armed drones are also used to try to target individuals. For example, one of ISIL's key leaders was killed in a drone attack in August 2016.

The practice of targeted killings using drones has been controversial. There are concerns about how many innocent people, including children, are also killed in drone attacks. Some experts think that there will always be someone to replace terrorist leaders when they are killed. Others suggest that by causing civilian deaths, the attacks are helping terrorist groups recruit more members.

THINK ABOUT IT

Data for US drone strikes in Pakistan from 2004 to 2016 showed that there were a total of 424 strikes. Up to 4,001 people were killed and up to 966 were civilians. Up to 207 of these civilians were children.

33

Chapter 5

WHAT'S BEYOND THE HEADLINES ABOUT DOMESTIC TERRORISTS?

Islamic extremist groups have dominated recent headlines with their international attacks. But security forces around the world also have to deal with "domestic terrorists". These groups use violence to intimidate for more local goals.

▲ Membership of the Ku Klux Klan in the US was at its height in the 1920s. They even held a march on the capital, Washington, in 1926.

THINK ABOUT IT

World governments have lists of terrorist groups and monitor people that might be linked to them. Why do you think it's important for nations around the world to help each other fight terrorism?

In the US, groups such as Black Lives Matter have staged peaceful protests in response to increasing hate crimes following the election of President Donald Trump.

◄

Racial and religious hatred

Racial tension in both the UK and the US has grown around two important votes in 2016. In the UK, people voted to leave the European Union, in a vote nicknamed "Brexit". Some people took this as an opportunity to commit race crimes against non-British people. Muslims and Jews — whether they were British or not — were also targeted. In the US, the election of President Donald J. Trump prompted some to express racial hatred. The country saw an increase in hate crimes against Muslims, Jews and African Americans.

On their own, these hate crimes are not necessarily classed as terrorism. But there has been a rise in the membership of terrorist groups such as the Ku Klux Klan (KKK). In the US, hate groups grew from 784 in 2014 to 892 in 2015. The KKK formed after the American Civil War (1861–1865). Members used violence and intimidation to try to prevent the newly freed former black slaves from gaining civil and political rights. By the height of its popularity in the 1920s, Klan members were also targeting Roman Catholics, Jews, foreigners, and Communists.

Membership of black separatist groups also grew rapidly in the US, from 113 in 2014 to 180 in 2015. Black separatist groups are against integration with other races and want separate institutions for black people. These groups are different from movements such as Black Lives Matter, which seek equality for blacks.

Nelson Mandela: from terrorist to president

In 1948, the white South African government introduced a policy that divided people into groups based on skin colour. The policy was known as "Apartheid", which means "apartness" in one of the local languages, Afrikaans. Apartheid discriminated against blacks, people of mixed race and Asians. It restricted what jobs they could do, what schools they could go to and where they could live.

At this time, a young black lawyer called Nelson Mandela was part of a group called the African National Congress (ANC). The ANC was trying to achieve the right to vote for blacks and people of mixed race. At first, the group tried peaceful methods of protest but in 1960 the Sharpeville massacre triggered a change of strategy. Twenty thousand black people had demonstrated at the Sharpeville police station in protest of Apartheid laws. The police eventually opened fire on the protestors. Sixty-nine people were killed and the ANC was outlawed.

Nelson Mandela gives a speech in 1961. ▶

Despite becoming the president of South Africa, Nelson Mandela was still on the US terrorist watch list until 2008. Some people within ANC had links with communism and that was enough to make the US suspicious.

Nelson Mandela went "underground" and trained for **guerrilla warfare** and **sabotage**. He was jailed in 1962 and given a life sentence for sabotage, **treason** and violent conspiracy in 1964.

A change of policy

In 1989, F.W. de Klerk became the president of South Africa and helped end the system of Apartheid. After 27 years in prison, Mandela was released in 1990, along with other political prisoners. In 1994, he was elected South Africa's president in the first election that was open to people of all races.

Nelson Mandela served as ▲ president of South Africa from 1994 to 1999.

THINK ABOUT IT

Nelson Mandela admits to using violence to try to gain civil rights for non-whites. He committed acts that were classed as terrorism. Was Mandela right to use violence to achieve greater freedoms?

The Troubles in Northern Ireland

Peace in Ireland is fragile. The 20th century has seen the use of violence by terrorist organizations because of disputes over territory. The situation was triggered in 1921 when the country of Ireland was divided in two after a war against British rule. The south became its own country, the Republic of Ireland. The north became Northern Ireland and remained part of the UK. But the opinions of people in Northern Ireland were passionately divided. The nationalists, or republicans, wanted an independent Ireland. This group of people was mainly Catholic. The unionists, or loyalists, wanted Northern Ireland to remain part of the UK. They were mainly Protestants and dominated the government.

Both sides in Northern Ireland had groups who used terrorist tactics to try to gain political change. These terrorist attacks were particularly bad in a 30-year period known as "The Troubles", which started in the late 1960s. Over 3,600 people from both sides were killed and over 50,000 people were injured.

In 1998, a car-bomb exploded in Omagh, killing 29 people and wounding 220 others.

▼

A lasting solution

The UK government realized that peace was never going to be won through military means. They tried instead to offer political settlements to put an end to the cycle of violence. The government would only work with groups it considered to be legal and not violent. So terrorist groups created political wings, such as Sinn Fein, which was linked to the terrorist group IRA.

The Irish Prime Minister ▲
Bertie Ahern said that "the spirit of democracy contained in the Good Friday Agreement will win out against all of the negative and destructive forces we have had to deal with over the years."

GOOD NEWS

After a number of failed peace agreements, the 1998 Good Friday Agreement finally put an end to The Troubles. Self-government was to be returned to Northern Ireland.

Many people visit sites such as the former Nazi concentration camp at Auschwitz to remember victims and learn from the mistakes of the past. ▼

How can we make a difference?

Making a difference in war and terrorism might seem to be beyond what most of us are able to do. Yet when we take the right lessons from the past, we can change the future for the better. For example, once details of the Holocaust came to light, people around the world were horrified. Many honoured the victims by promising to never forget. Yet groups with racist beliefs similar to those that fueled the Holocaust continue to exist to this day. It is important to learn about the past and why wars and conflicts have happened. Those who understand the past can better understand why current conflicts are happening. They can then make informed decisions that will potentially make the world a better place for everyone.

One way of remembering those who lost their lives in world wars is through annual remembrance services. In these services, many people in the UK wear poppies, after the poppies growing in the battlefields of WWI. They do this to show gratitude for those who gave their lives for the cause of freedom.

Be informed

ISIL is like no other group in its use of social media to inspire followers and recruit new fighters. Researchers found that ISIL supporters tweeted more than 23 million times over a ten-month period. We live in a time where the world has more, and easier, access to information than ever before. But that doesn't mean all information is accurate. It's important to understand the source of the information you are reading. Does the writer have an interest in persuading you to think in a particular way? Is the source factually correct? Can you double-check the information with other reliable sources?

It is important for everyone to learn how to think critically about information that is available online. ▲

Conclusion

The way wars have been fought over the 20th century and into the 21st has changed. We haven't seen wars on the scale of WWI and WWII, largely due to the fear of nuclear weapons. The world's superpowers know that the use of nuclear weapons would have a devastating impact on the whole world. Though they have not engaged in direct conflict, they have been involved in many other wars such as the Vietnam War, the Iran-Iraq War, multiple wars in Afghanistan and the Syrian Civil War. In some cases, these wars have fueled the rise of the very terrorists Russia and the US are currently fighting.

These makeshift memorials were placed to remember the victims of the 2016 terror attacks in Nice. ▼

◄ Leaders at the UN hope to play a key role in preventing the spread of violent terrorism.

Ending terrorism

Putting an end to terrorist activity is more difficult than resolving a conflict between two nations. Terrorists deliberately use tactics that are unexpected and cause fear. However, experts try to prevent future attacks by using statistical patterns to predict what a group is likely to do next. In 2016, the UN announced their plan of action to prevent violent extremism. Their plan contains over 70 recommendations. These include empowering women and youth, engaging communities, and strengthening good governance, human rights and the rule of law.

Ban Ki-m, former UN Secretary General:

"Missiles may kill terrorists. But I am convinced that good governance is what will kill terrorism."

TIMELINE

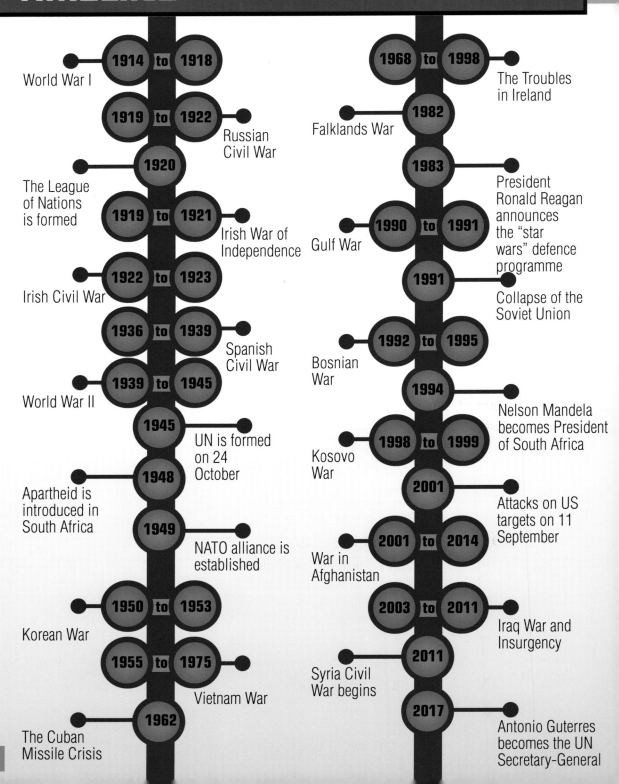

1914 to **1918**
World War I

1919 to **1922**
Russian Civil War

1920
The League of Nations is formed

1919 to **1921**
Irish War of Independence

1922 to **1923**
Irish Civil War

1936 to **1939**
Spanish Civil War

1939 to **1945**
World War II

1945
UN is formed on 24 October

1948
Apartheid is introduced in South Africa

1949
NATO alliance is established

1950 to **1953**
Korean War

1955 to **1975**
Vietnam War

1962
The Cuban Missile Crisis

1968 to **1998**
The Troubles in Ireland

1982
Falklands War

1983
President Ronald Reagan announces the "star wars" defence programme

1990 to **1991**
Gulf War

1991
Collapse of the Soviet Union

1992 to **1995**
Bosnian War

1994
Nelson Mandela becomes President of South Africa

1998 to **1999**
Kosovo War

2001
Attacks on US targets on 11 September

2001 to **2014**
War in Afghanistan

2003 to **2011**
Iraq War and Insurgency

2011
Syria Civil War begins

2017
Antonio Guterres becomes the UN Secretary-General

GLOSSARY

apartheid means "apartness" in the language of Afrikaans. It was the name for a South African policy where people were treated differently depending on the colour of their skin

atomic bomb weapon that uses nuclear power to create massive destruction

CIA Central Intelligence Agency in the US

civilian person not in the armed services or the police force

coalition group of nations or governments who join together for a certain goal

Communist person practicing communism, a political system in which there is no private property and everything is owned and shared in common

democratic using the political theory of democracy. This is where people believe that governments should be voted for in elections.

dictator person who has absolute power

ethnic represents origin of birth rather than nationality

globalism treating the whole world as a place to operate economically and politically

guerrilla warfare fighting by small groups of irregular fighters against larger regular forces

ideology beliefs associated with a certain group or way of thinking

nuclear weapons weapons that use nuclear power to create massive destruction. Nuclear weapons include atomic bombs and hydrogen bombs.

radiation particles given out by the nuclear bomb which can make people ill or even kill them

sabotage deliberately damage or destroy something

Soviet Union group of communist countries. The full name was the Union of Soviet Socialist Republics (USSR).

treason betray one's country

trench long narrow ditch dug by soldiers as a place to shelter from enemy shots

truce agreement to stop fighting

United Nations (UN) a group of countries that works together for peace and security

World War I (WWI) (1914–1918) the war between the Central Powers (Germany, Austria-Hungary, and Turkey) and the Allied Powers (mainly France, Great Britain, Russia, Italy, Japan, and the United States)

World War II (WWII) (1939–1945) the war in which the United States, France, Great Britain, the Soviet Union and other countries defeated Germany, Italy, and Japan

FIND OUT MORE

National news websites and newspapers are a good way of keeping up to date with the latest information about topical issues.

Websites

www.iwm.org.uk
Imperial War Museums in London, Manchester and Cambridgeshire

www.jewishmuseum.org.uk/Home
Jewish Museum, London

www.nationalholocaustcentre.net
The National Holocaust Centre and Museum, Nottinghamshire

www.nms.ac.uk/national-war-museum
National War Museum, Edinburgh

Books

Life on the Western Front (Remembering World War I), Nick Hunter (Raintree, 2014)

Nelson Mandela (Against the Odds), Cath Senker (Raintree, 2015)

Nelson Mandela: Revolutionary President (Inspirational Lives), Kay Woodward (Wayland, 2014)

Resisting the Nazis (Heroes of World War II), Claire Throp (Raintree, 2015)

INDEX